TARTAN
DESIGNS
COLORING BOOK

MARTY NOBLE

DOVER PUBLICATIONS, INC.
MINEOLA, NEW YORK

A tartan is a woven pattern of overlapping stripes of various sizes and colors. Although the pattern itself originated in central Europe around 3000 B.C., the tartan is almost always associated with Scotland's kilts and culture. In Scottish history, particular tartans—distinguishable by color and stripe size—were used to represent families, towns, districts, individuals, and even corporations. Today, the popularity of the tartan has become so widespread that it can be found all over the world in the clothing items and blankets that are commonly referred to as "plaid."

This seemingly simple pattern allows for infinite possibilities for color usage and technique, thus making another ideal addition to Dover's *Creative Haven* series. The pages are unbacked so you can experiment with whatever media you like, and perforated for easy display!

Many of the patterns in this book were inspired by *Scottish Tartans in Full Color*, by James Grant (Dover: 0-486-27046-7).

Bibliographical Note

Tartan Designs Coloring Book is a new work, first published by
Dover Publications, Inc., in 2014.

International Standard Book Number

ISBN-13: 978-0-486-78625-4
ISBN-10: 0-486-78625-0

Manufactured in the United States by RR Donnelley
78625002   2015
www.doverpublications.com

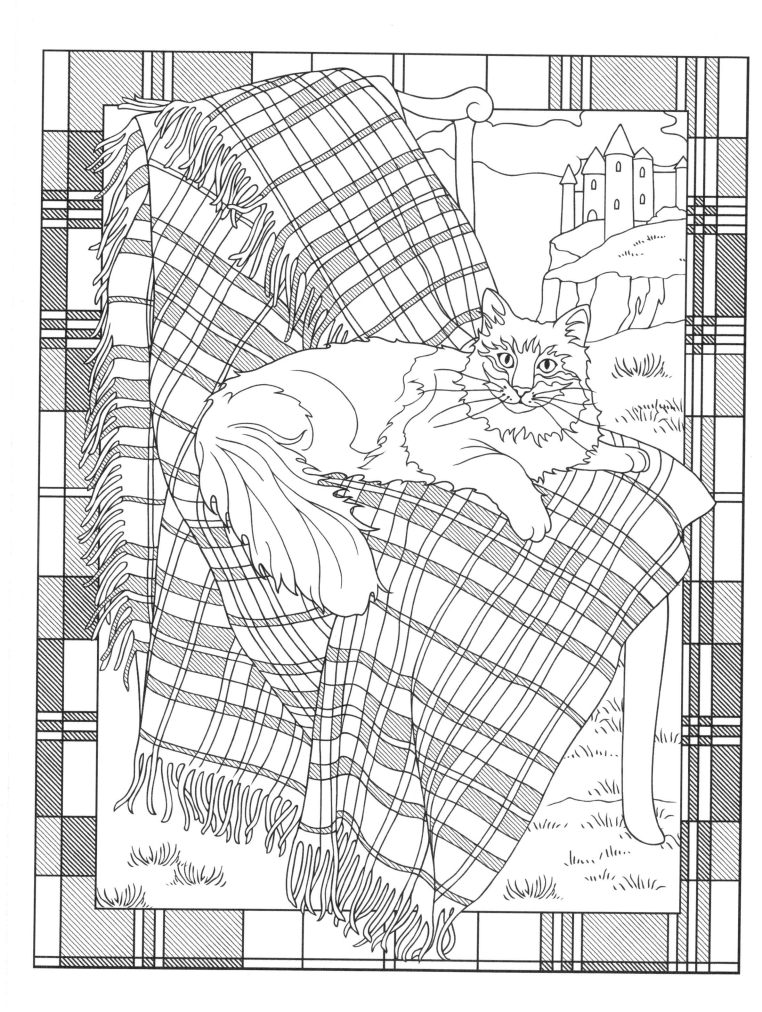

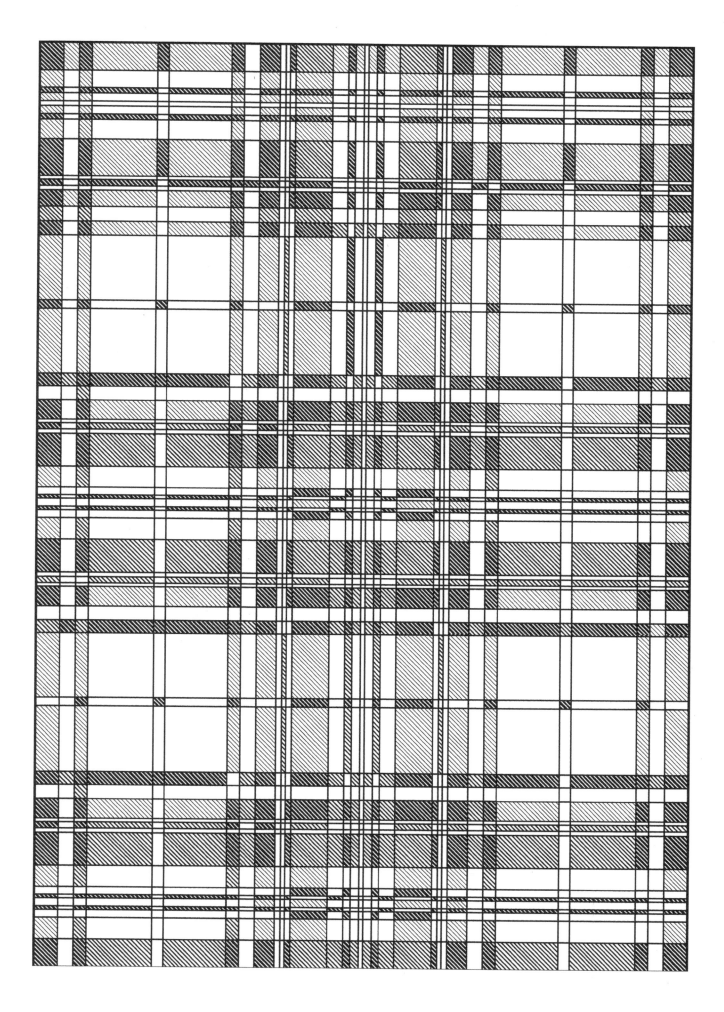

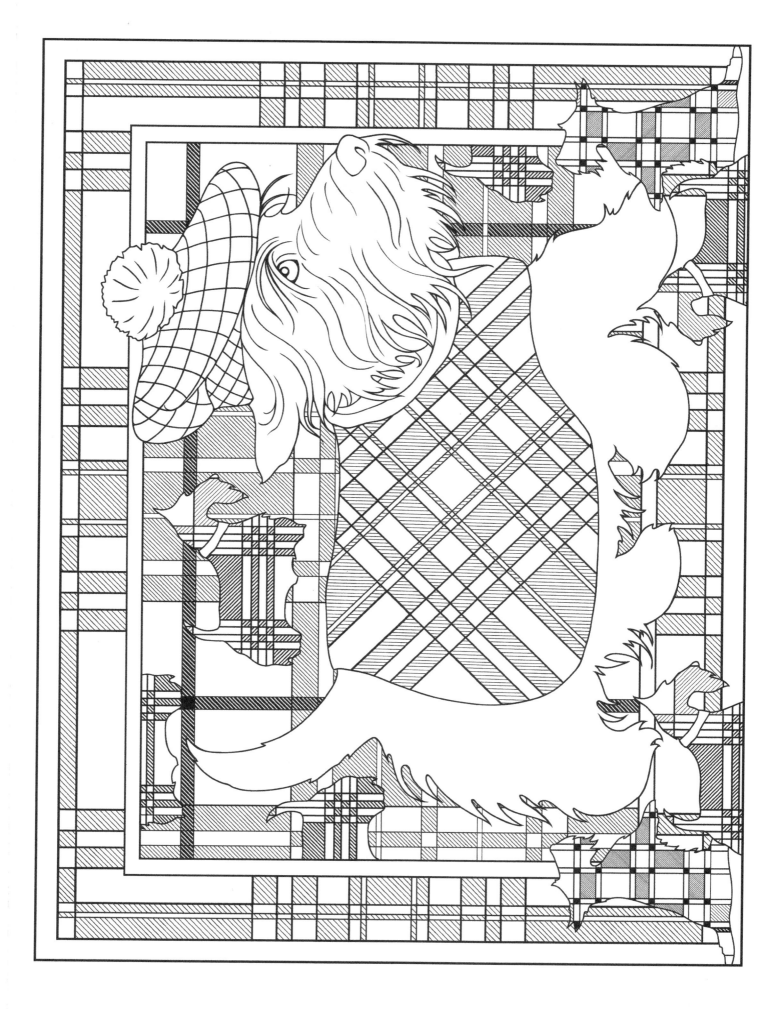

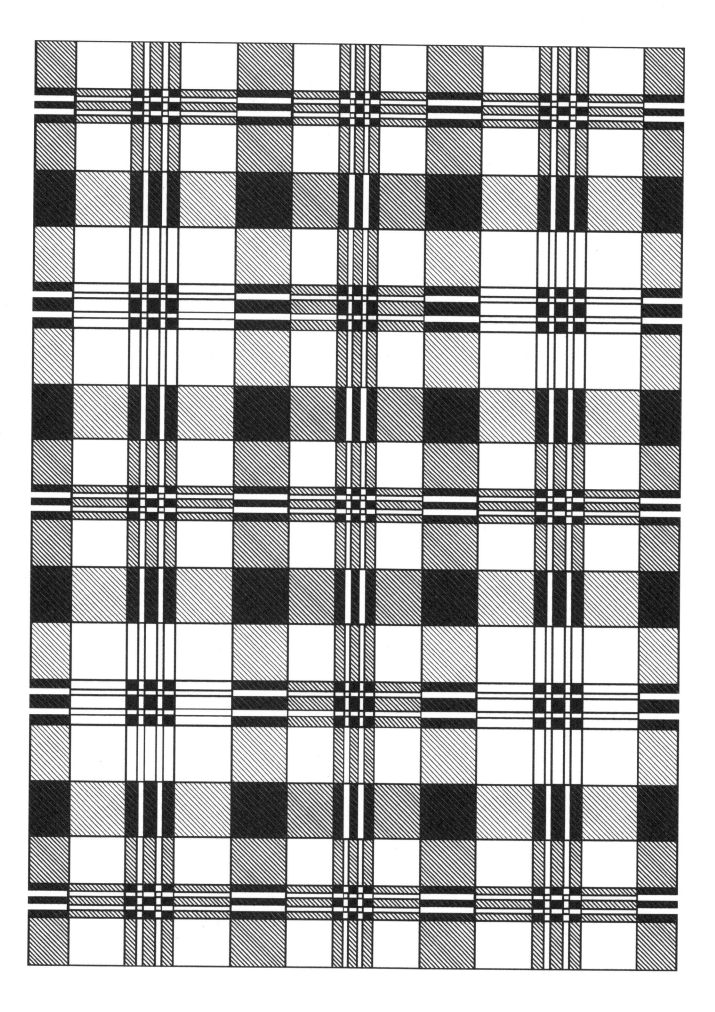

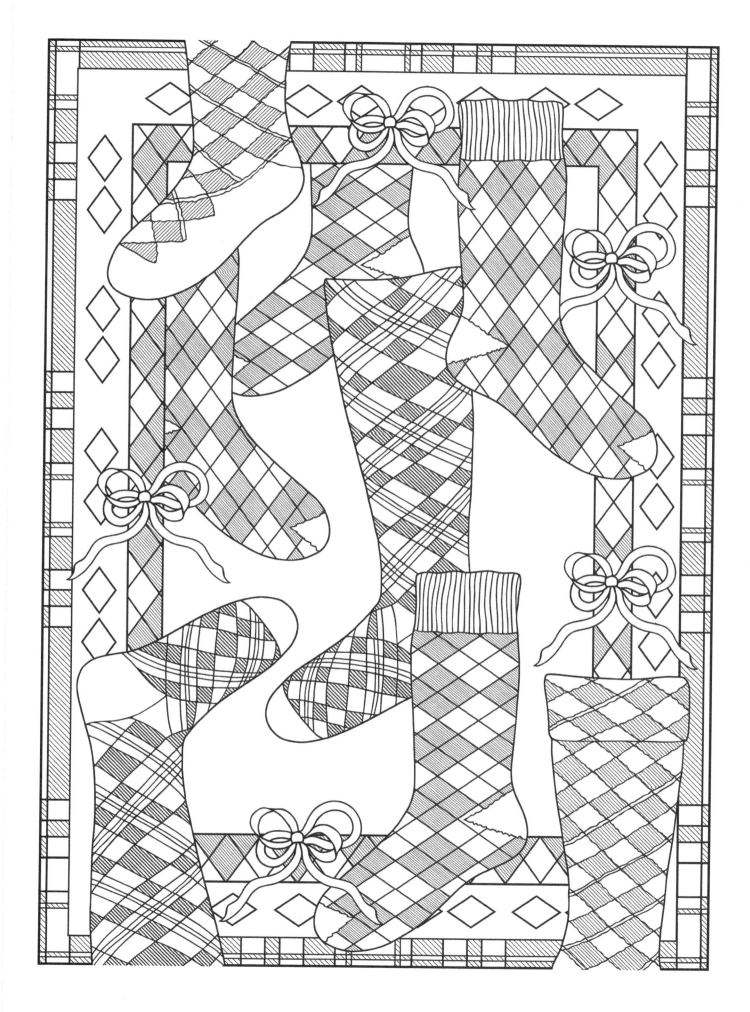

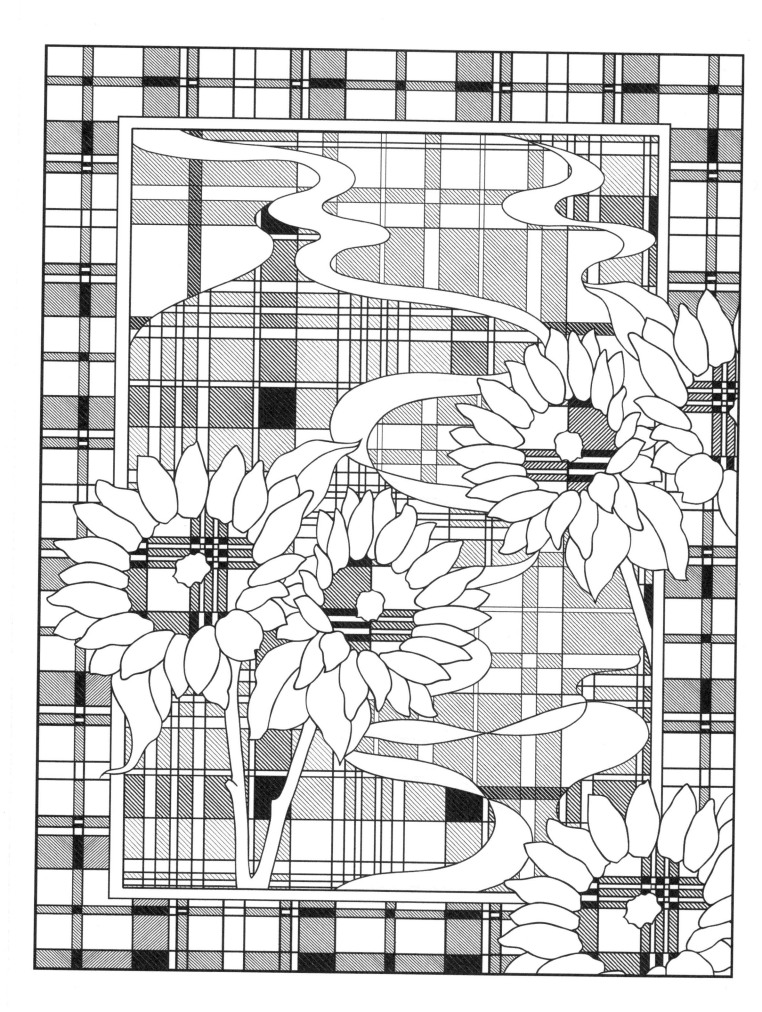

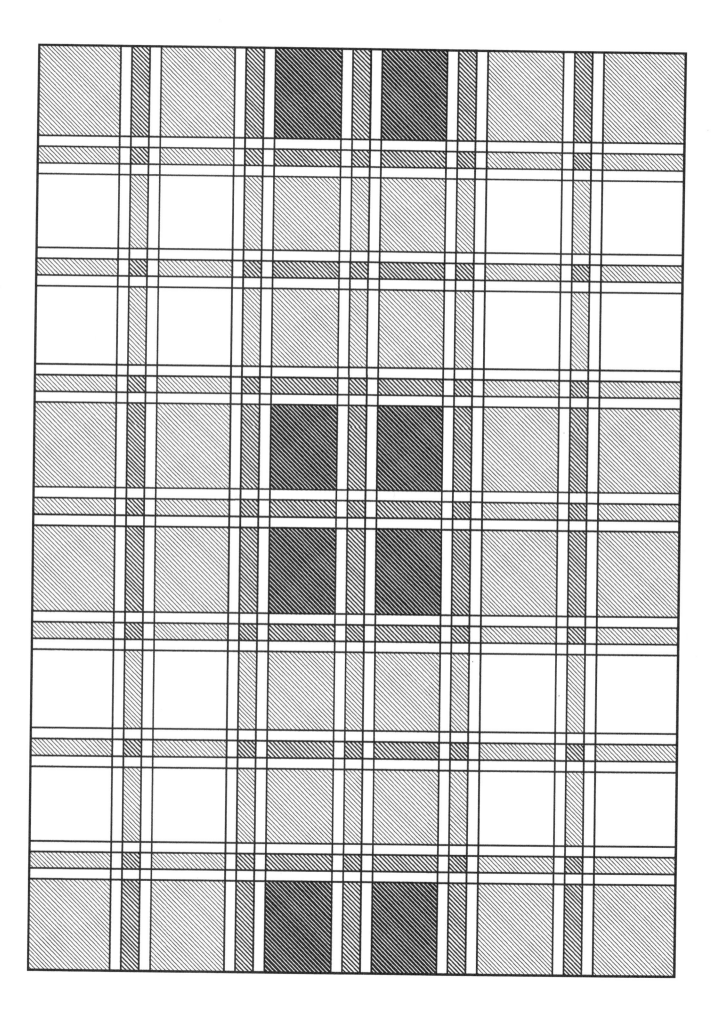

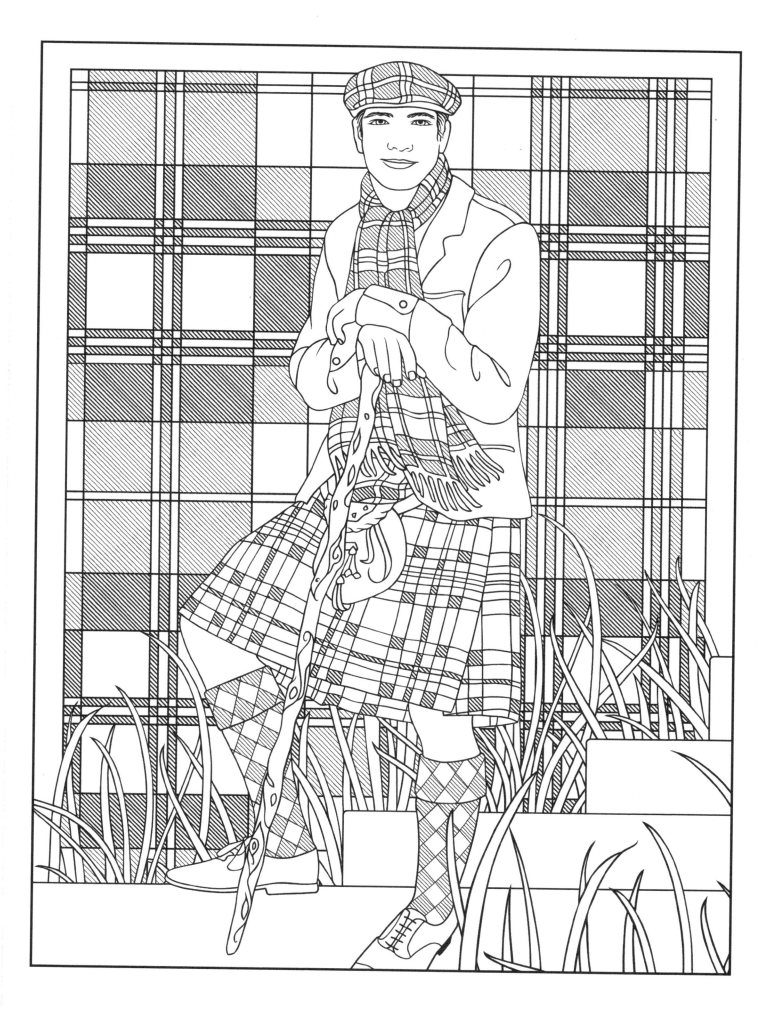

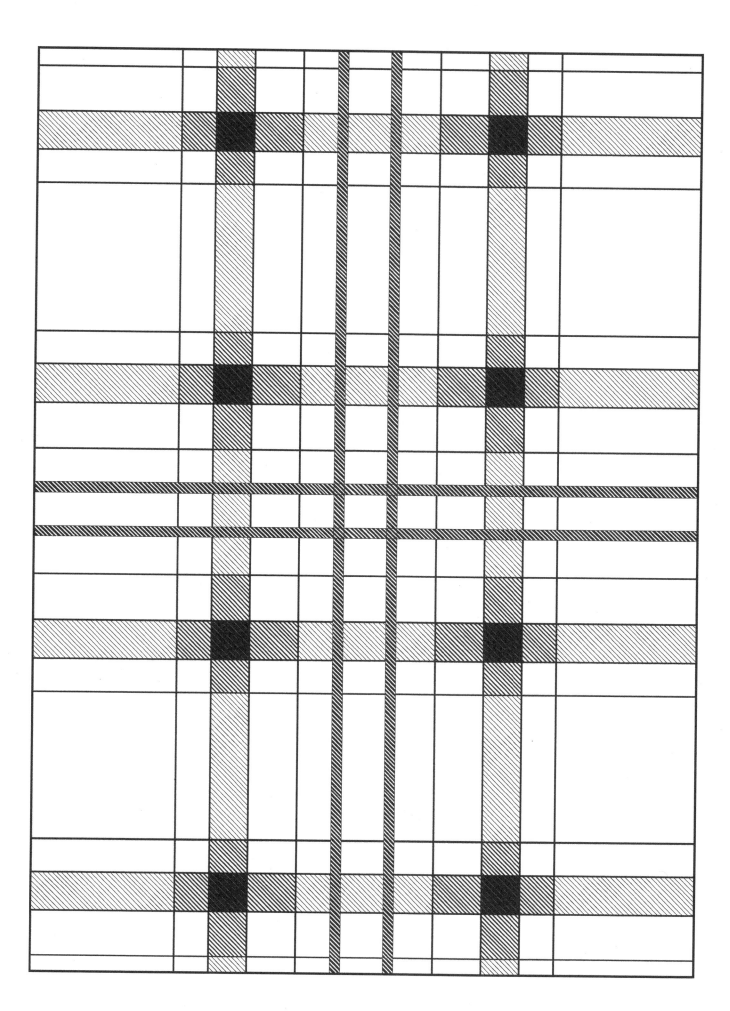

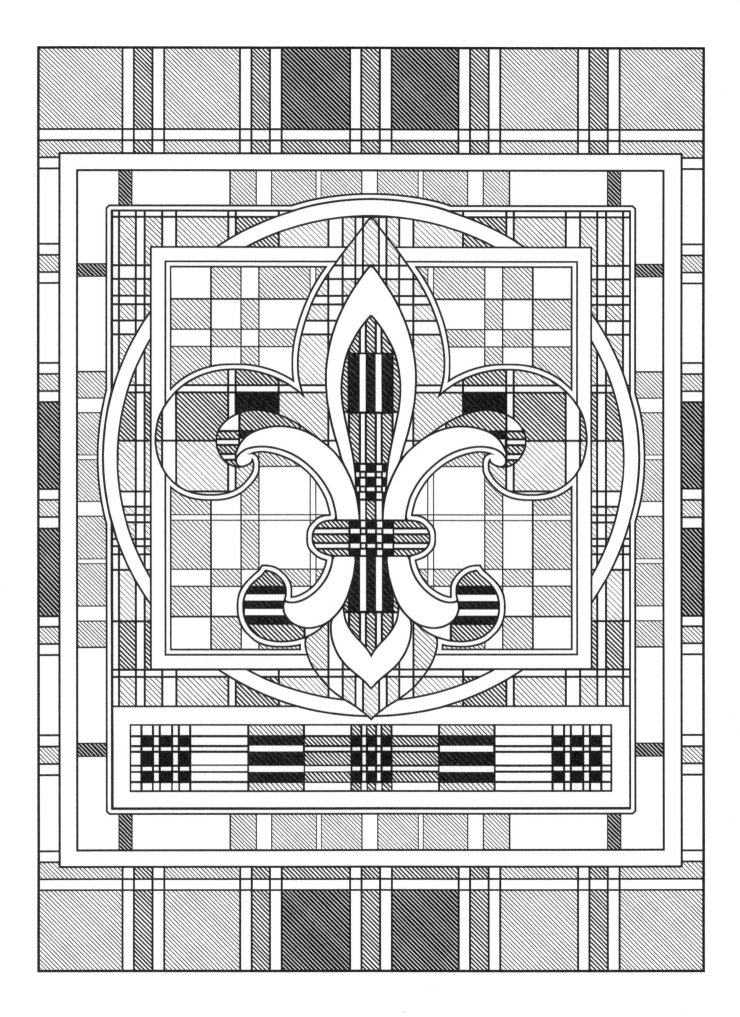

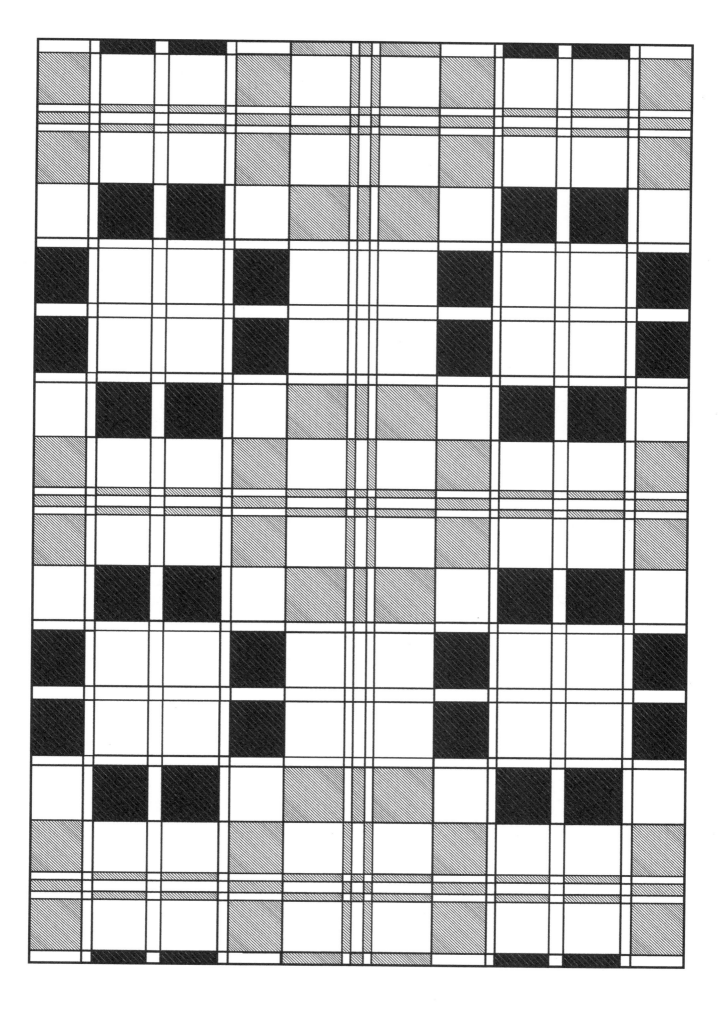

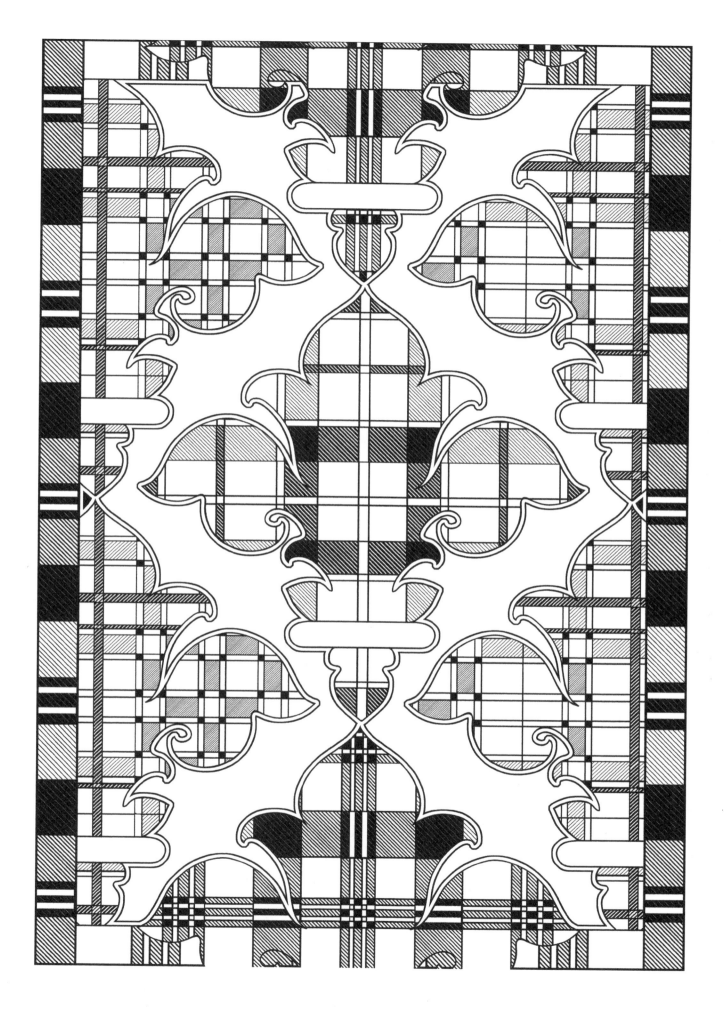

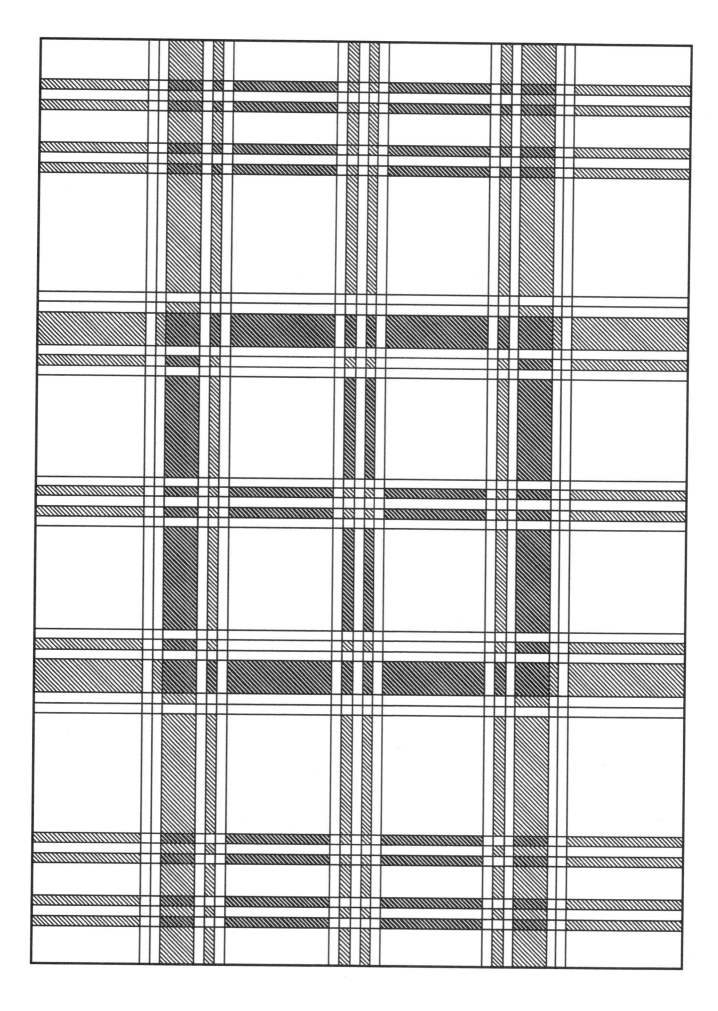

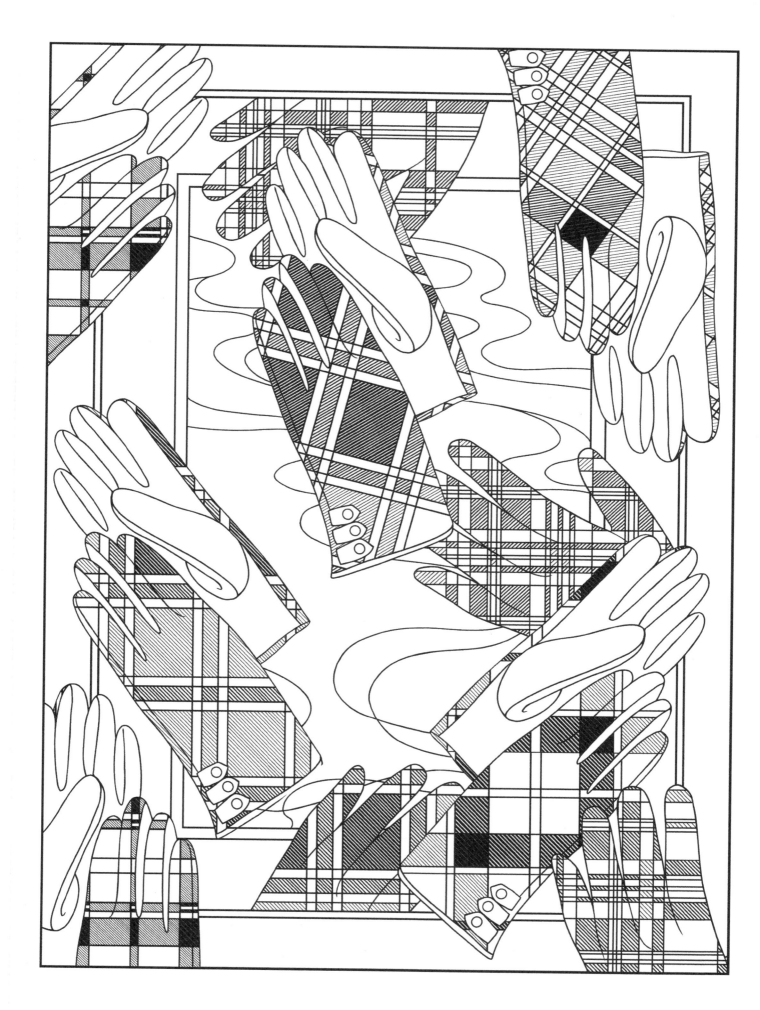

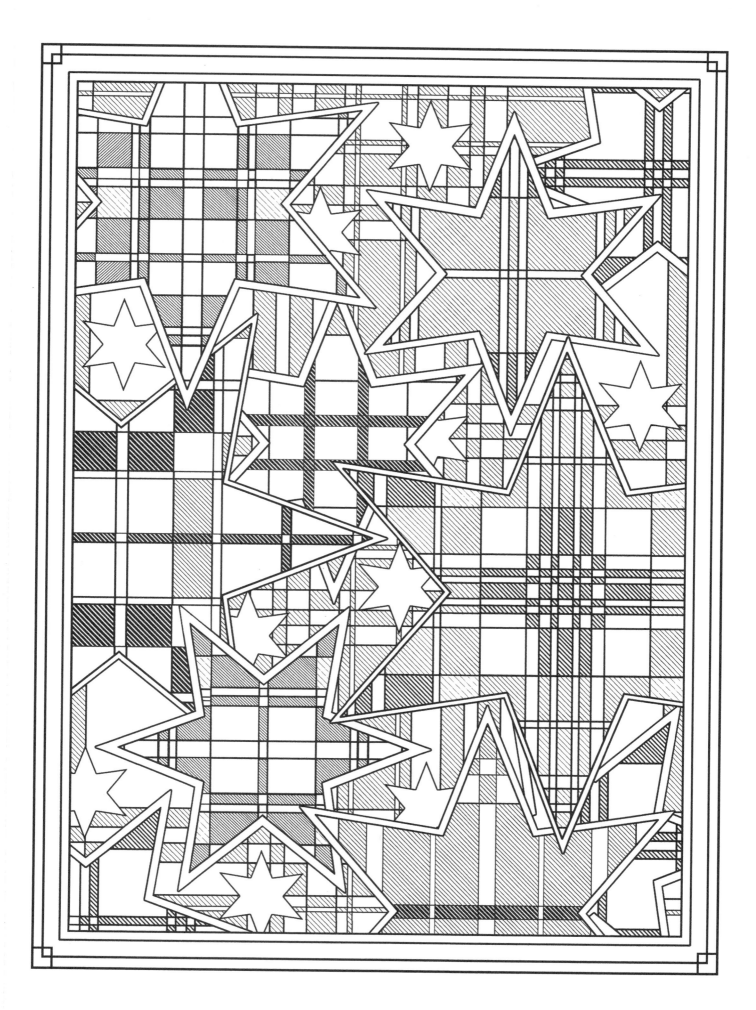

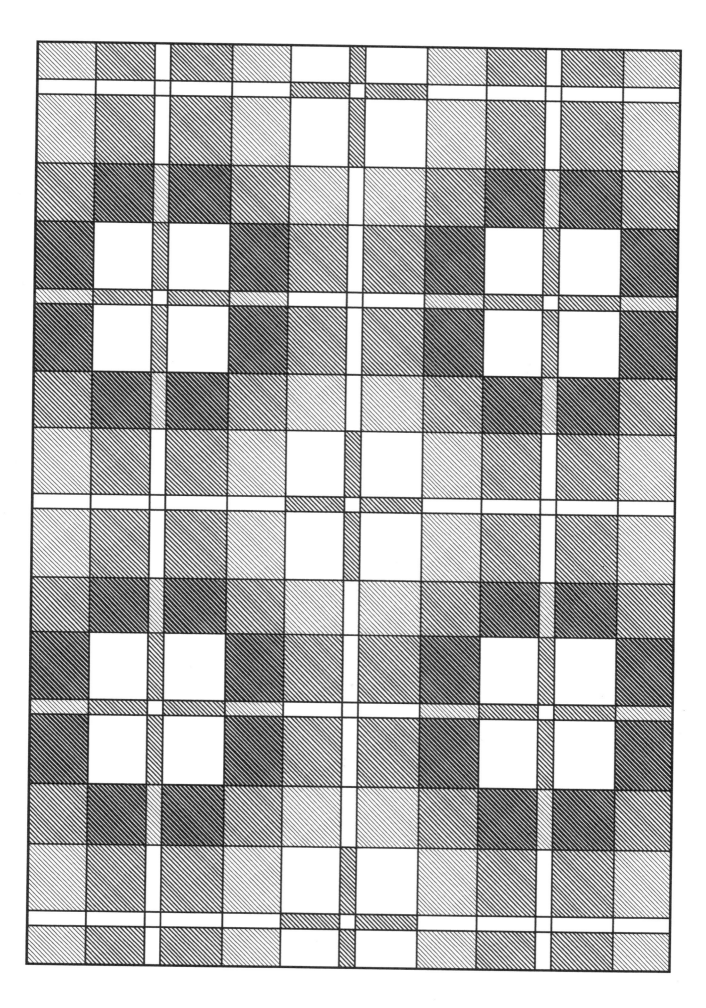

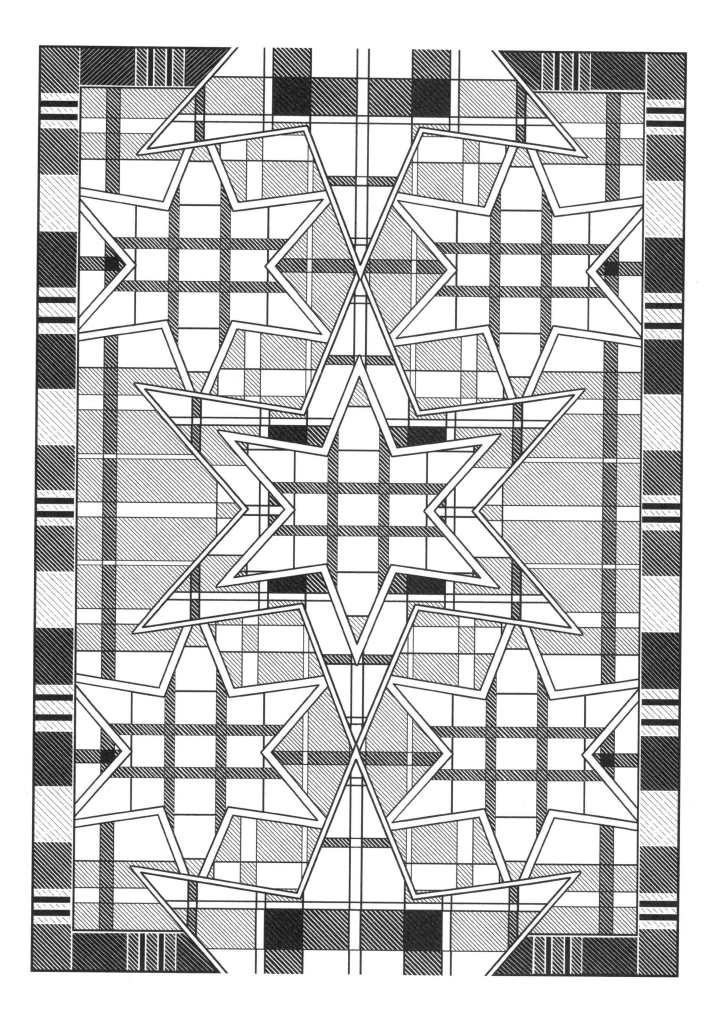

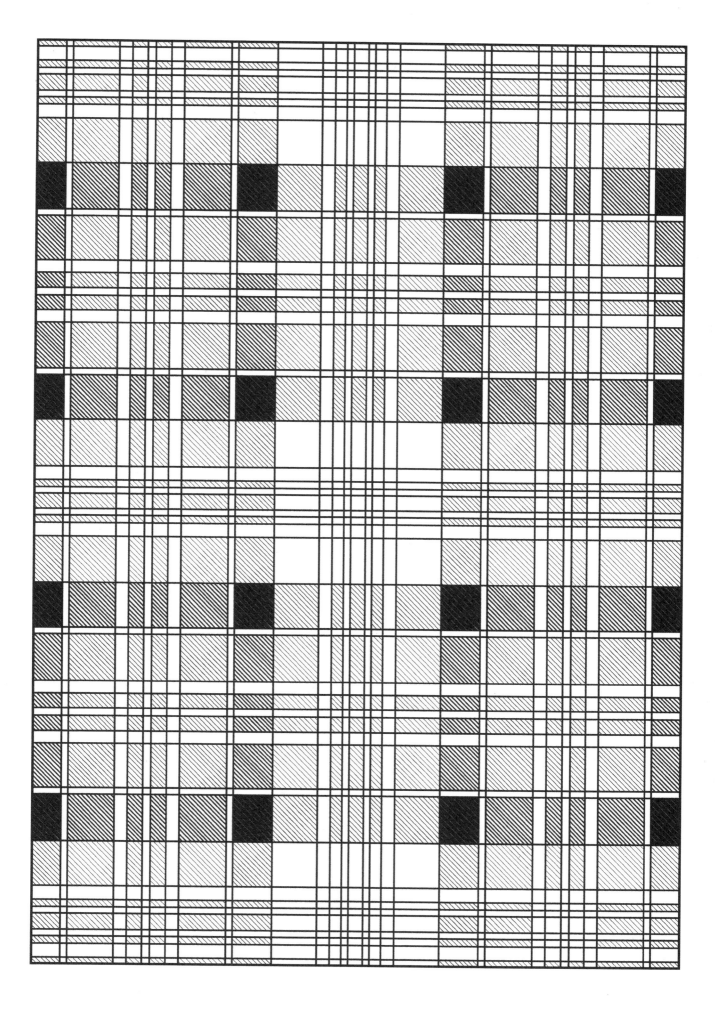

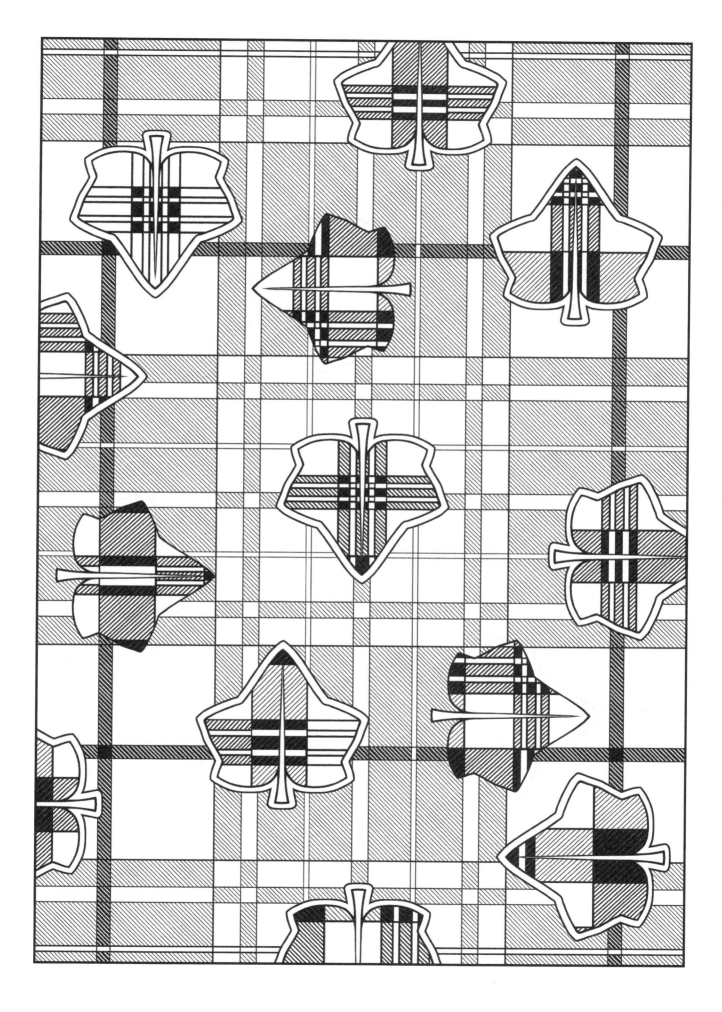

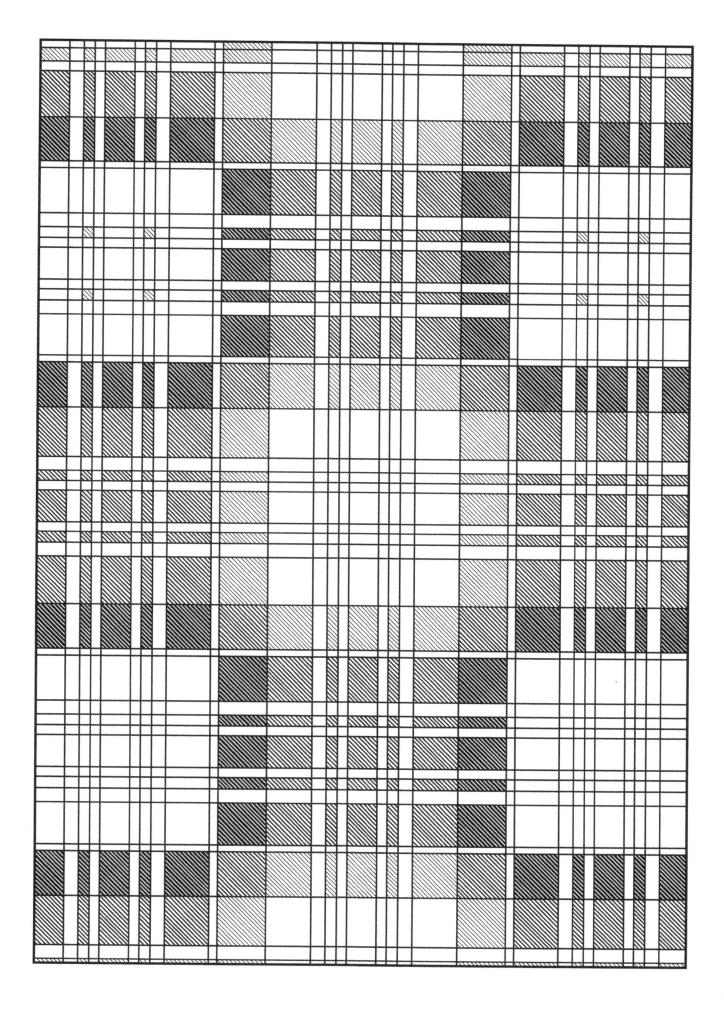

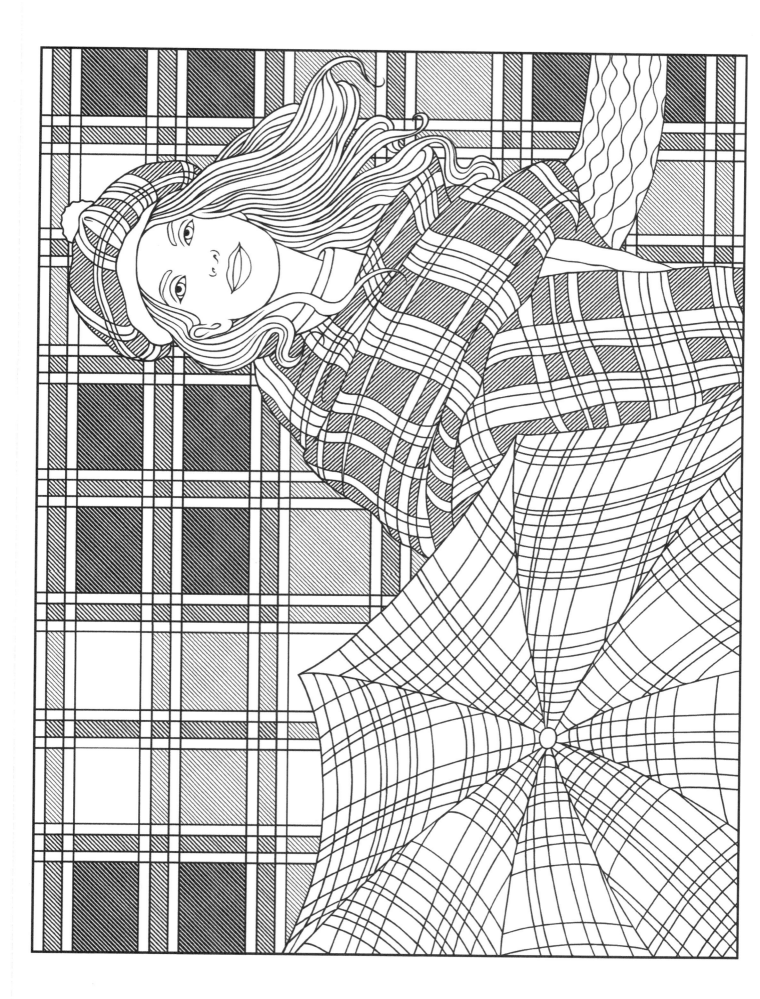

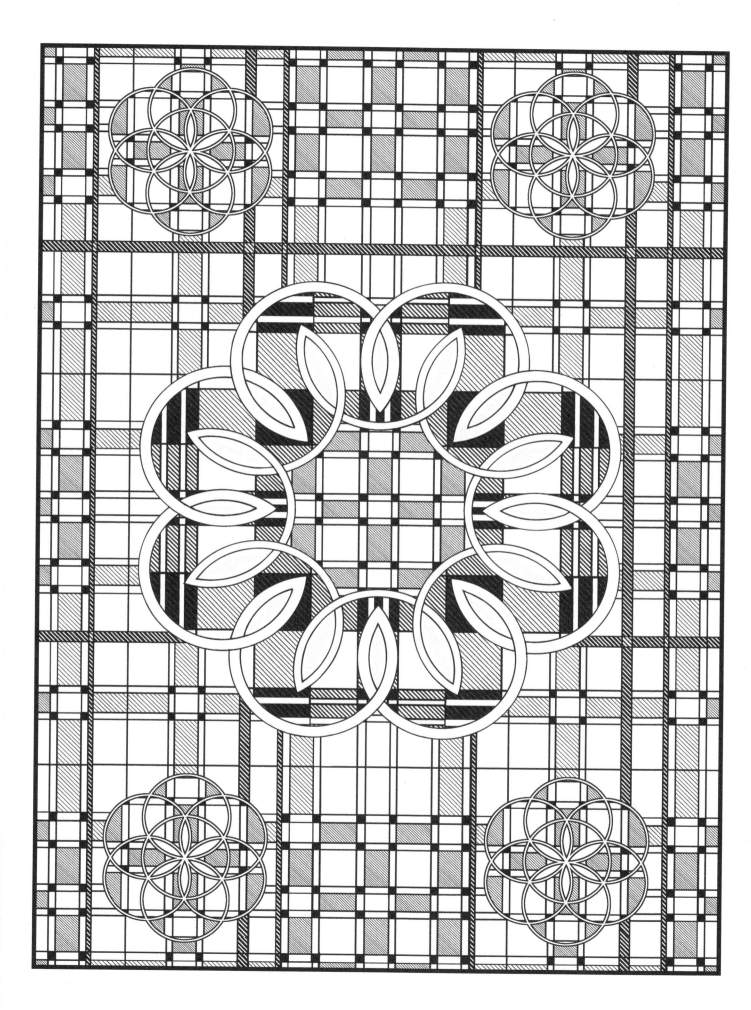

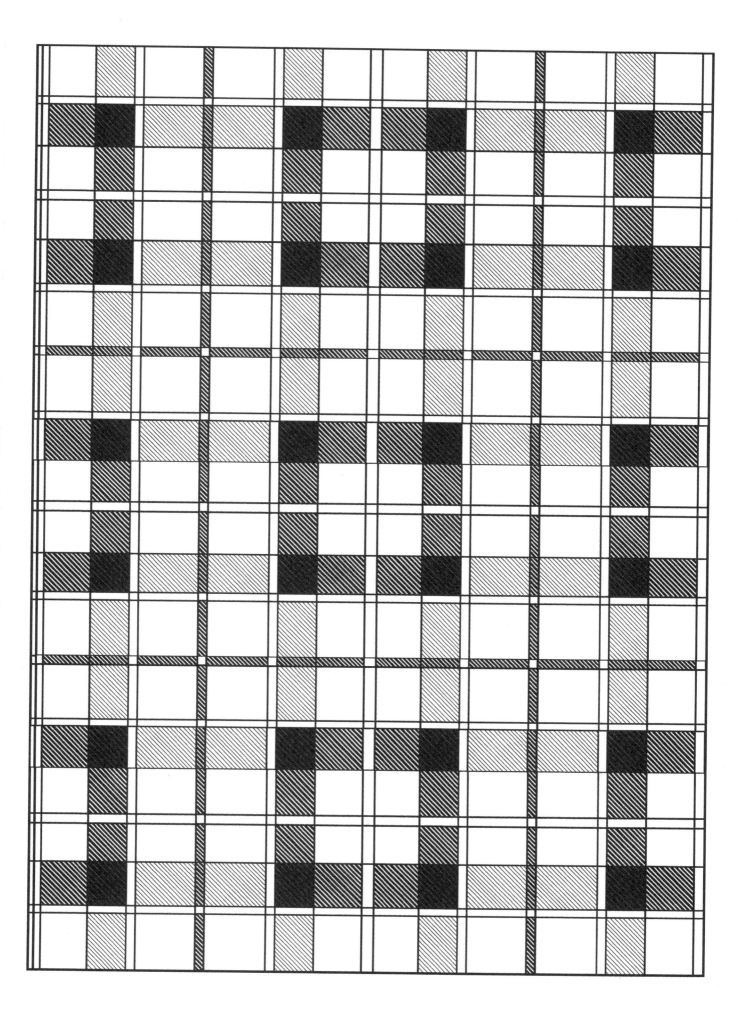

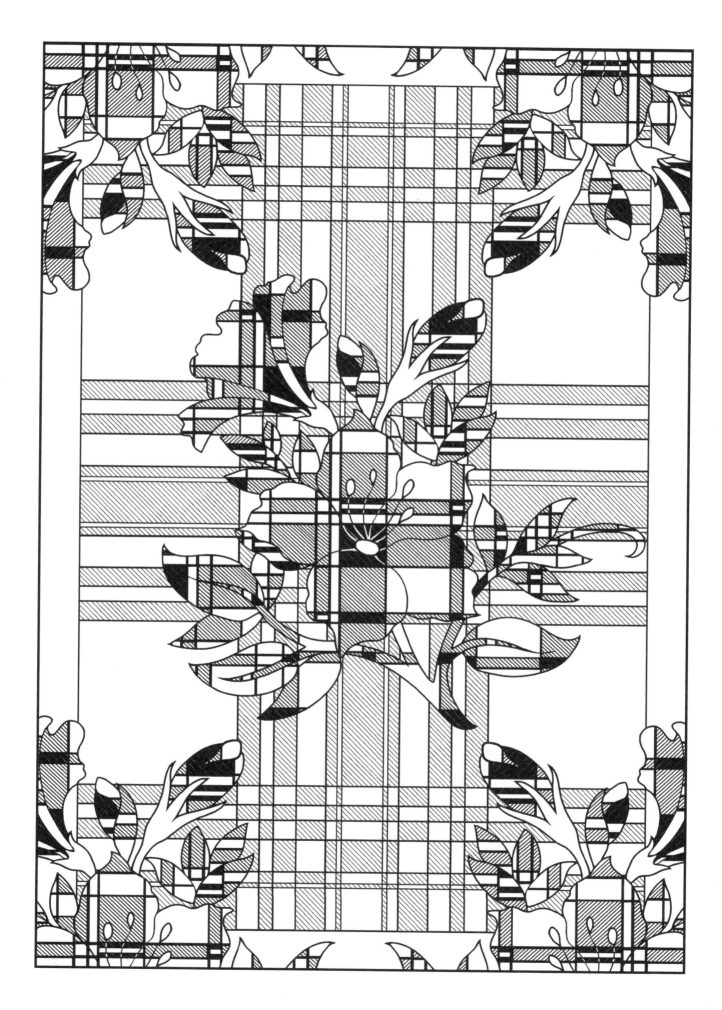

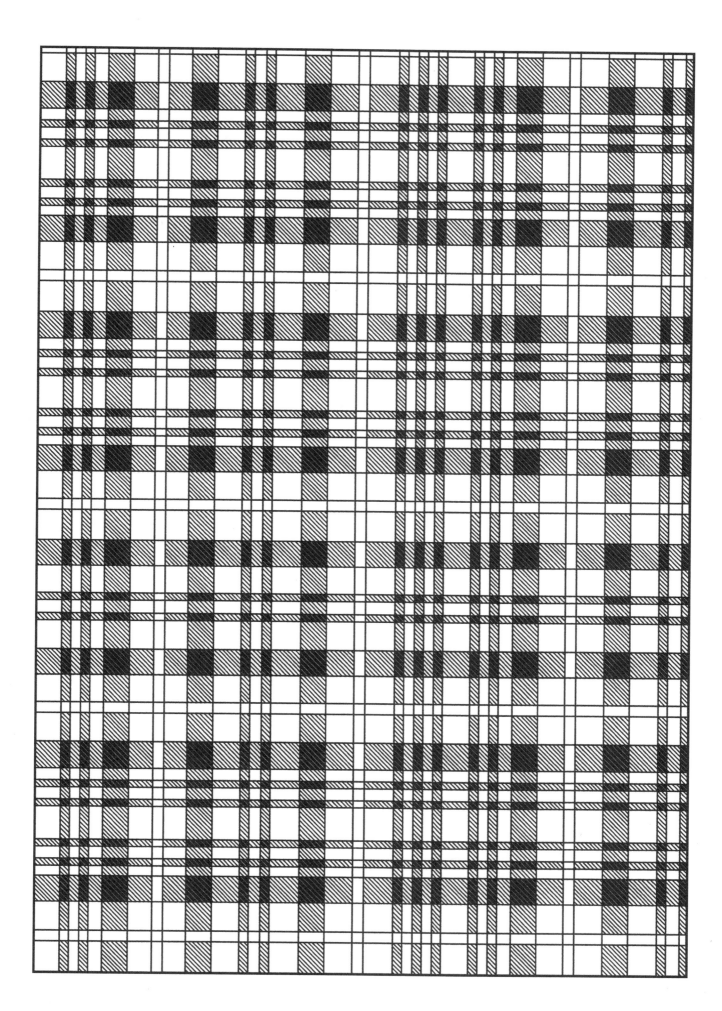

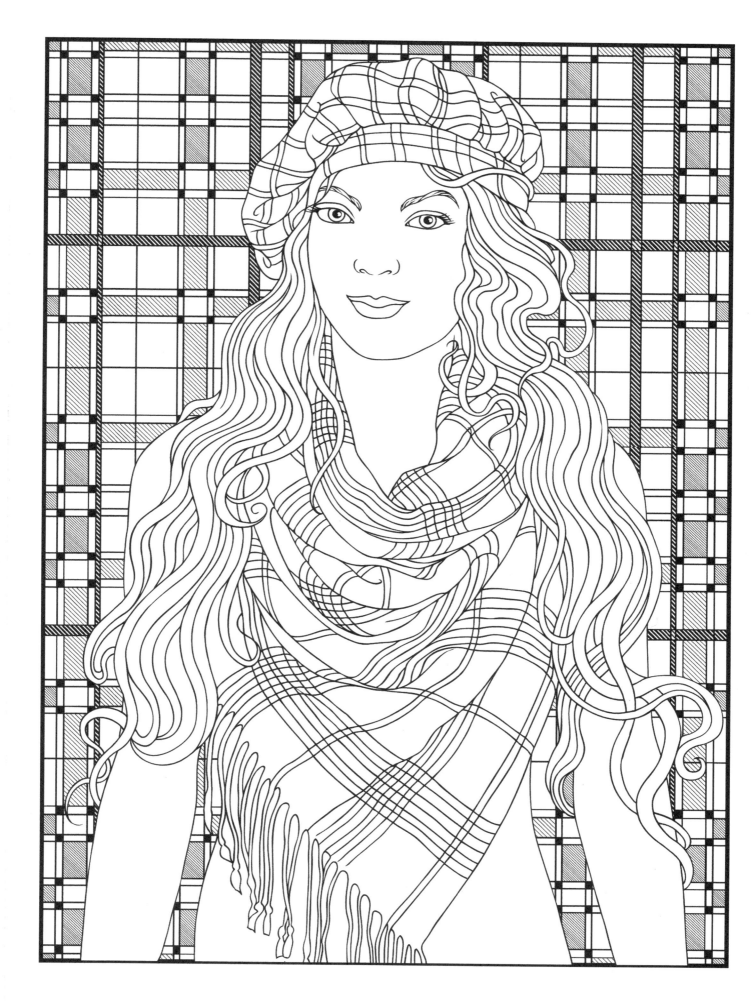

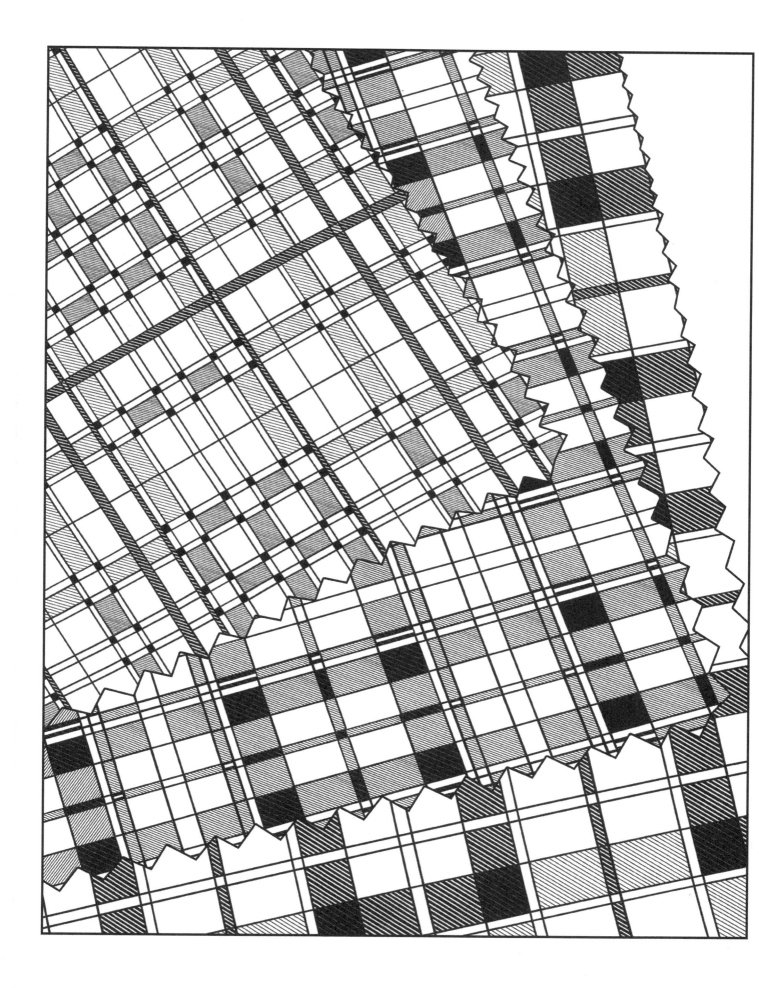

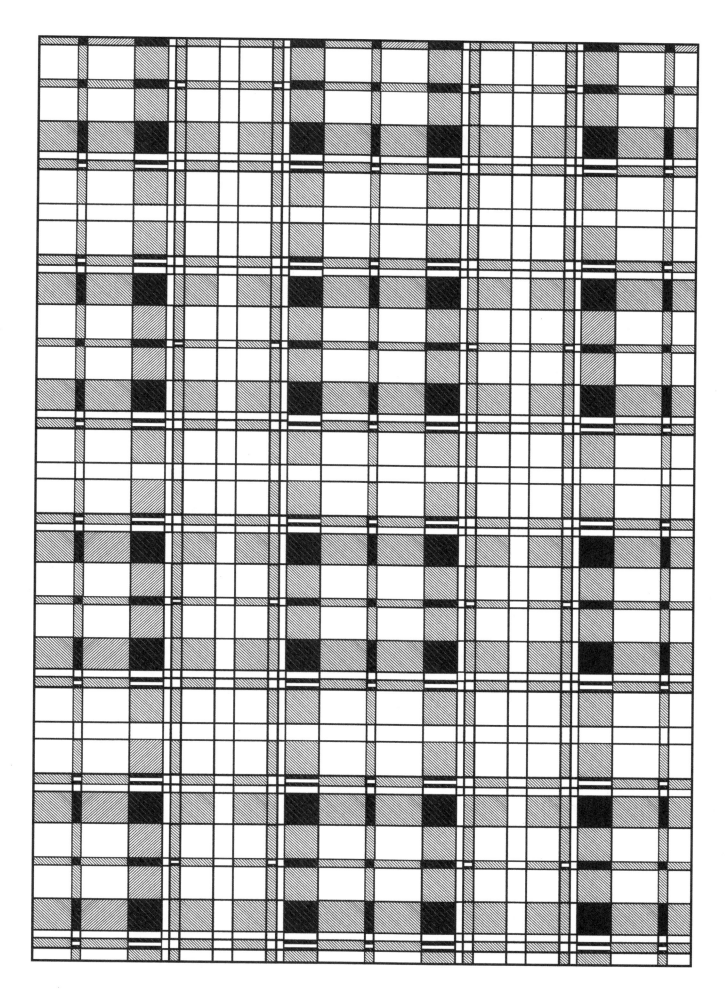

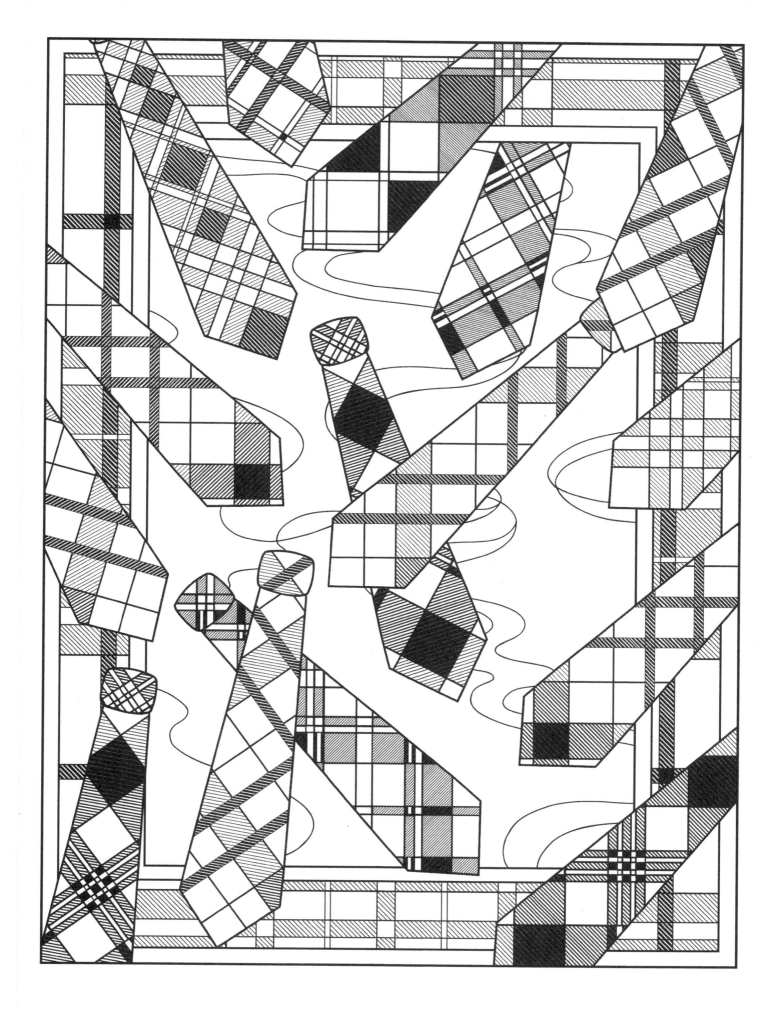

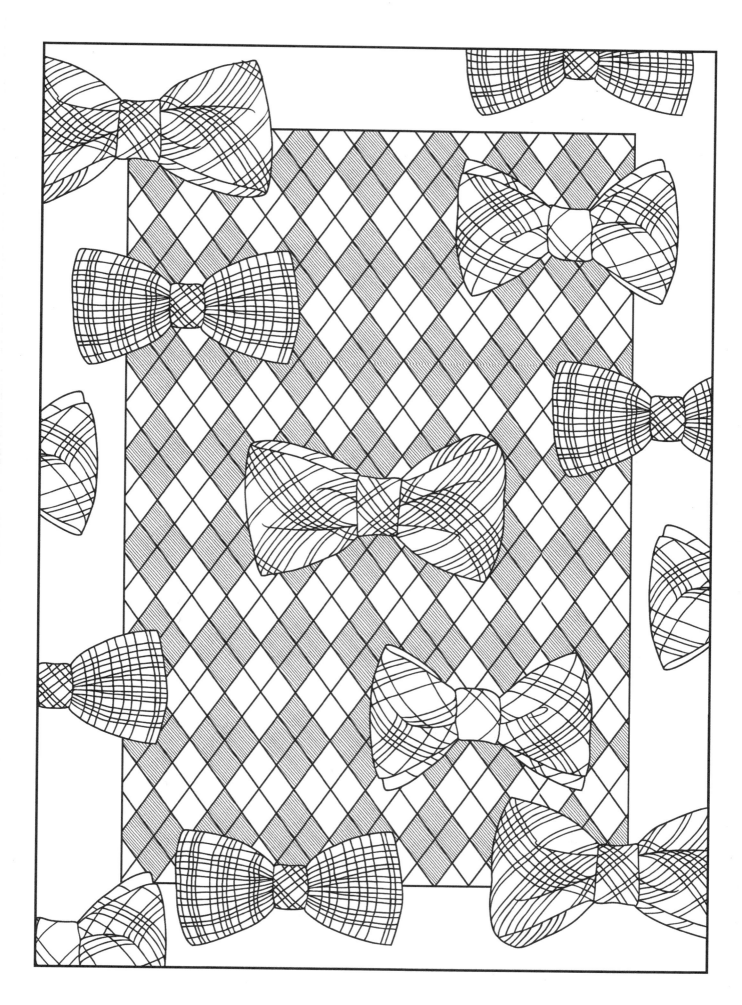

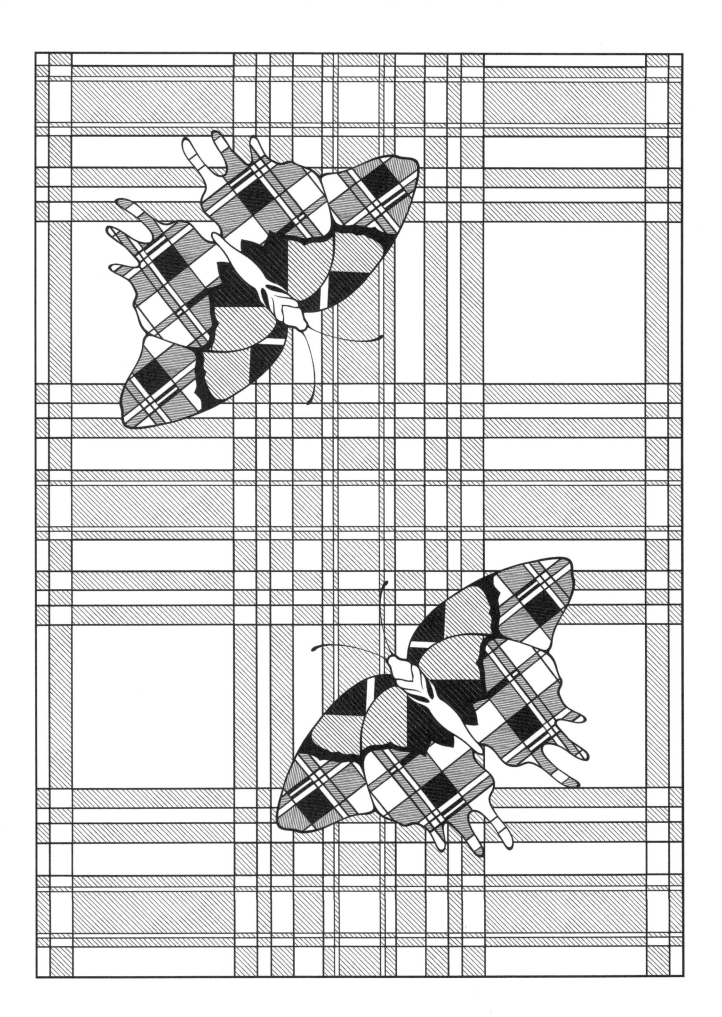